and you, Helen

and you, Helen

DERYN REES-JONES

with images by Charlotte Hodes

SEREN

Seren is the book imprint of
Poetry Wales Press Ltd
Nolton Street, Bridgend, Wales

www.serenbooks.com
facebook.com/SerenBooks
Twitter: @SerenBooks

The *'And You, Helen'* project, part of which this book reflects, was
commissioned by the Ledbury Poetry Festival, where it was performed in 2014.

Text © Deryn Rees-Jones, 2014
Images © Charlotte Hodes, 2014

ISBN 978-1-78172-172-8 (hardback)
ISBN 978-1-78172-218-3 (limited edition)

A CIP record for this title is available from the British Library

 The publisher works with the financial assistance of the Welsh Books Council

Designed by Roger Walton Studio
Set in Filosofia and Gill Sans

Printed by Akcent Media Ltd in the Czech Republic

CONTENTS

AND YOU, HELEN

And you, Helen, what should I give you?
So many things I would give you
Had I an infinite great store
Offered me and I stood before
To choose. I would give you youth,
All kinds of loveliness and truth,
A clear eye as good as mine,
Lands, waters, flowers, wine,
As many children as your heart
Might wish for, a far better art
Than mine can be, all you have lost
Upon the travelling waters tossed,
Or given to me. If I could choose
Freely in that great treasure-house
Anything from any shelf,
I would give you back yourself,
And power to discriminate
What you want and want it not too late,
Many fair days free from care
And heart to enjoy both foul and fair,
And myself, too, if I could find
Where it lay hidden and it proved kind.

Edward Thomas

And you, Helen, what should I give you?
So many things I would give you
Had I an infinite great store
Offered me and I stood before
To choose. I would give you youth,
All kinds of loveliness and truth,
A clear eye as good as mine,
Lands, waters, flowers, wine,
As many children as your heart
Might wish for, a far better art
Than mine can be, all you have lost,
Upon the travelling waters tossed
Or given to me. If I could choose
Freely in that treasure-house
Anything from any shelf,
I would give you back yourself,
And power to discriminate
What you want and want it not too late,
Many fair days free from care
And heart to enjoy both foul & fair,
And myself, too, if I could find
Where it lay hidden and it proved kind.

AND YOU, HELEN

'Between the terrific noise of the guns I can hear two hedge sparrows making love.'

Edward Thomas

(to be spoken by a female voice)

PROLOGUE

Can the loosestrife make us a home?
Can the skylark, stuttering, sing
and be known to us? Can the bee, creaturely,
dodging the breeze? Can the dragonfly
with her wings of glass? Can the bitter leaf
and sweet grasses, grass seeds,
meadowsweet and chickweed. Can the ants
and woodlice, windblown burrs?
Can the spider, assembling herself,
pull threads of silver one to another?
Can celandine, catkins, an orchard
bound in mistletoe? Can the moth,
alert at our edges? Can a butterfly
rising and gliding in the powdery nettlebeds,
can the shadow of the oak tree
casting itself from green to black?
Even as the sky darkens can the hare,
stilled at the field's edge, nervy, watching,
bring us an answer? I answer yes.
And love hunkers down,
shows us her great mercy.

1

At first, she sees nothing.

Darkness rubs at her – star-blasted, dream-filled – knocking her
                                                    sideways from love,

out of sleep. None of this knows itself. Slow. Forming. Now it is
morning and so there's a shift, when dark is an opening. A heartbeat
on darkness. Pulse. *Pulse.*

This is her mind: connecting with feeling

with thought   with a memory   memory of thought.
Loosestrife. Nettles. She fumbles in spaces, can sense
in the half-light
the breath of her children.

Her body takes root. Her body takes hold.

Roses blacken in a jug at the bedside. Ash in the grate
                                        remembers its fire.

Now it is morning. Yet still there is nothing.

Nothing

but a space beside her.
            Nothing,
                but a space inside.

2

The oak tree knows the field,

                the bend of its shadow to the grass.

    It knows the sun's path -- passage of blackcap, starling, rook --

how to clutch a song and nest it in leaf. It knows the ant that

      labours up grass blades; a stag beetle glinting, passage of worms.

The tree --- surrenders --- its shadow to shadows. Oak tree and field

      converse in the shadowgrass. Here is how shadows bend, here

        is where birds rise.

                Birds   rise   up.

(Had the night known its own self --- darkness ----

it would have opened wide its mouth, afraid.)

Two men walk across the field. Her heart's beat like a missed step.

August wears ghost selves. And the shadow of one

                keeps on walking into shadow.

While the shadow of one

      lies down.

                    Pause.

Moth flutter

      like shadow broken loose

        carving grey in the moonlight.

First you hear rain, then you imagine it, seeing how rain might

      drum at its brokenness.

        Drums inside.

A man feels the dark field singing through his bones.

She feels it, too. Rain singing. Love singing. Here, now,
are its broken lines. Here, in a heartbeat,

the white explosion.

A body lies, thickening with mud. And the dead who are long gone
open up their mouths.

The rain. The field. Every small thing it owns.

3

Where he is, stumbles.

Although she can imagine him, pulls lovingly a thread - - - - - - -
his voice - - - - - - -
- - - - - - - -
silence

breaks in the listening,
widens, stretches.

A hare quivers like an unearthed wire.

Hush.

While the field moves she's complete in her listening.
Rain on the roof makes eaves a dull listening.

Then thunder dulls, and the sky splits.
She's dreaming of journeys and trains through the darkness.
Elder, dogwood, flaming maple.

- - - - - - - - - - pulls at a thread.

4

As this old tin bowl holds water for washing, it holds, too,

the memory of water.

As her body holds the memory of - - - - - - - - - -, she holds, too.

As a gun holds the memory of its firing,
as the earth soaks up water, sends it skyward;

as the skylark - - - - as the fieldfare, sparrow, blackcap, rook - - - -
as her body holds his body,

as their slow, deep movements - - -
he holds too.

As milk burns in the breast, remembering the tug of - - -
as their bodies are a bridge, and children call to her
out of their sleep - - - - - - - - - -

as her collar bone, as her pelvic bone, as her - - -
everything

holds

as the horses - - - - - - - -
as the - - - - - -
as the - - - - - - -

as she wakes from a dream
as shrapnel, as mud.

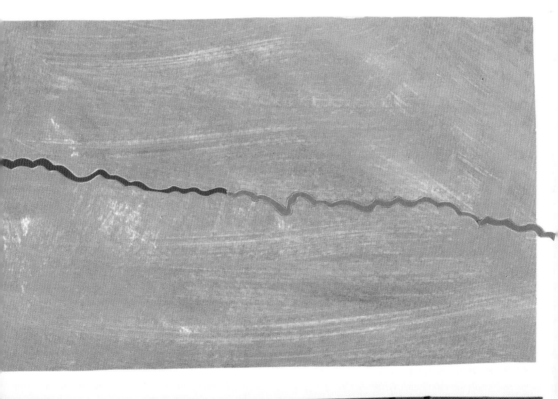

5

Where she is, stumbles. Her fingers move to the edges of her body,
negotiate the space at her clavicle; she holds the full weight

of her breast in her hands.

She cannot feel much more than this.

When she wakes, she reaches for the space. Is it always like this?

Each step, each step - - - - - - - -

as if each bare foot on the wooden stairs

might suddenly explode.

So field edge touches sky edge.

So a pair of sparrows squabble in the corn stooks.

Somewhere, between the greying field and the dusk dark,
between grass song, her whisperings, and tree song,

the talking of the leaves,

a body hangs in a moment.

Here is the moment between living and dying,
the space beyond and the space inside.

She stretches out her limbs and - - - - - - - - - -

There is a conversation taking place.
The space beyond the space inside.

6

Does the breeze pull a thread of hair across a brow?
Does the movement of the blood around the body

       stoppered by the earth's stop

                    run to a halt?

Do the lungs expand, after death, to this?

And is silence then its own sound?

Does she wait now for an exhalation?

Does a wheeze of breath come at the very end, overdue?
Does a wren caught beneath a hedgerow suddenly appear?

Fieldfare, sparrow, rook.

There's blood at the throat. *Whose throat?*

His body is perfect. Only his heart,

as if caught in the split of a second,

              catching its breath.

He gives her a look. *Pause.*
The skies light up. Is this the way she might imagine him?

Poems feather in his pocket.

Birdsong. Here, is the stillness of - - - - - - - -

Robin or redstart, called palely to his palm.

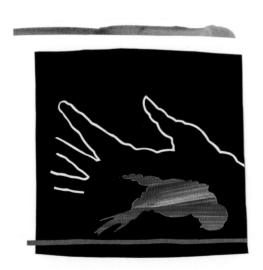

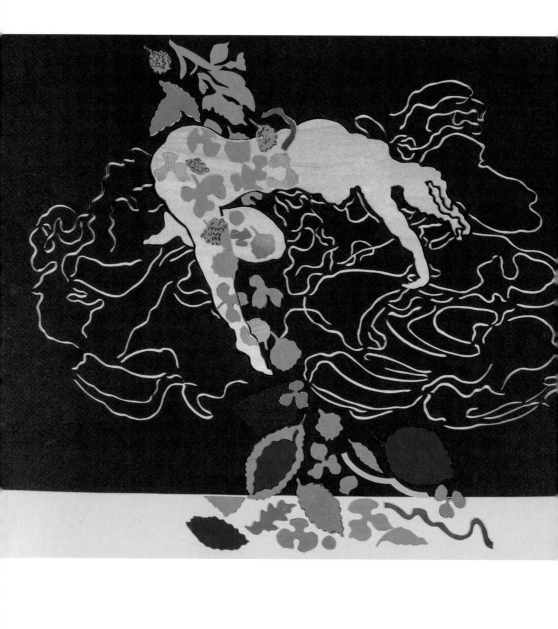

7

The memory of a memory. That last night returns to her. Fragments
melting in nudges of firelight.
His hand touches, without somehow touching,

> any human part of her.

> It is like this.

> - - - - - this slow gorgeous climbing and

gathering,

> this entering, this being inside.

White clover, yellow bedstraw, milkwort.

She drops a glass. And now her face, as if something at her heart

had spilled. Or the crack, singing like an ice floe in darkness,

> widens   holds.

What she holds,
>   she holds for their children. But now there is breakage.
The terrible shifting ocean of herself, let out.

8

Loosestrife, nettles. She'd unbuttoned her blouse,
letting her clothes fall loose to the waist,
then pool in a circle - - - shoulderstaps, underclothes - - -

She makes his body, as she guides his hands, a poem.
The sun a covering, the sky a covering. Their two bodies

in one movement

                      a poem in the grass.

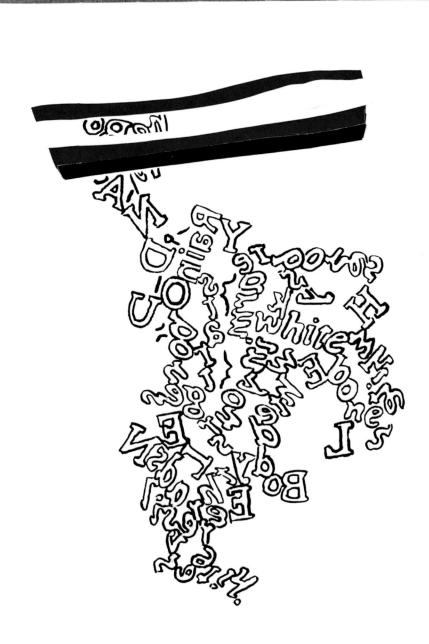

9

She remembers the day he turned tight on his heel,

took a gun in his hand to walk out to the woods.

The children's eyes blackened

like wounds in the darkness

                and her own heart split.

She wonders at the fury of endurance.

Where to place love?

Sinew   curve

edge   vein

Love

      cooks, digs, sews, binds, smoothes, irons, cleans,

                    wrenching from tiredness, dirt,

                              a tenderness.

When they lie together in the night, it is something like this --------

Pulse.

Rain furies,
      dances, sings.

If he sees the world through her eyes, then she sees the world through his.

10

He has gathered her up in his old great coat.
Can he carry her, she wonders, like the girl she was,
in his officer's coat, with his freshly razored hair.

Mosses grow on the furzy green; her red dress tears
like a wound, in a wound.
He has gathered her up and will sing to her

under the shadow of the deep-breasted oak.
Listen! This is the sound of his tread on the stairs.
He has gathered her up.

My arm in yours, my hand in your pocket.
You must walk, he laughs, with her hand in his pocket,
as if in your dreams.

And the dead who are long gone
open up their mouths.
Let us open up our lips. Let us show forth our - - - - -

Star-blasted, dream-filled.
White clover, yellow bedstraw, milkwort.
She opens her mouth to a dark field.

She opens her mouth
                    to a thousand leaves.

11

The oak tree knows the field.
She walks now, in its shadow. Nettles, meadowgrass.
All, now, that has travelled between them:
sweat, semen, blood, milk, tears.

Leaf shadow touches grass shadow.
A child mutters in the breakages of sleep.
First you hear rain, and then you imagine it.
She dances with him. Leaf shadow touches grass shadow.

And you, Helen?
She begins -

> *When I walk I walk with*
> *the white shock of an explosion.*

> *When I love*

> *When I walk I walk with*
> *their clean white bones*

(We hear the song of the thrush)

IMAGINING HELEN THOMAS

Oh do come back and be happy with me once
more. I'm sick to death of the loneliness eating my
heart out with anxieties and lost hopes. But don't
come till the rain comes. I have a superstitious
feeling that with the rain good will come all round.
This drought is unnatural and unkind, though I do
love the sun and the blue sky of it. But the rain and
the sweet smell of wet earth would bring I feel
relief to the soul of me. So dearest stay away as long
as you can, and come striding home with a jolly
'cooee' for us across the valley and three children
in your arms all of a bustle, and a kiss for me when
they can give us a moment, and then a meal, and a
long evening of calm talk. That is my picture. Oh
let it all come true! Or is it like the washing in the
Jordan difficult because of its simplicity?

*Letter from Helen Thomas to Edward Thomas,
September, 1911*

* * *

I first encountered Helen Thomas twenty-five years ago when I took down a Faber and Faber edition of Edward Thomas' *Selected Poems* from a friend's bookshelf, opened it at random, and read the poem 'And you, Helen'. It was a funny coincidence at the time: the friend to whom the book belonged was recently divorced; his ex-wife was called Helen. I sensed then that his love of Edward Thomas came not only from his own identification with Edward's self-laceration and melancholy but with his own failed marriage. At twenty I knew very little about Edward Thomas the poet, and had only a vague sense of Georgian poetry as Modernism's poor relative. But the poem caught me as much with its ability to become such an object of identification for someone close to me, as it did with its music and the awkwardness of the emotion it was expressing. Who was this woman whose identity was so plainly spoken? What was the nature and the quality of the gift that the poem was giving? There seemed, even in its generosity and honesty, its sadness and its apology, also an undercurrent of control and cruelty to the poem. Helen's presence has no doubt nudged silently away at me as I have come to know and love Edward Thomas' poetry. And you, says the poem, somehow sending the reader away. Not you, reader, but Helen.

* * *

Helen Berenice Noble was born on July 11th, in 1877, at 13, Moscow Drive, Liverpool, the second daughter of James Ashcroft Noble and Esther Lunt. The street in Old Swan is ten minutes from my house in the city centre, and I realise as I look at the birth certificate, that Helen is an exact contemporary of my own great-grandmother, who was also born nearby. The Noble family did not stay in Old Swan for long, and after a losing a child in the diphtheria epidemic, moved to a large Victorian villa with a garden in Birkdale, which was then a suburb of the coastal town of Southport. When Helen was about five years of age, and as James Noble's literary career continued to blossom, the family moved again, finally leaving the north-west for the suburbs of south London.

Helen Berenice. That second name adds something exotic and dashing. Helen of Troy. Helen, mother of Constantine, St Helena. Helen, shining light. Berenice. The name of so many of the queens of Egypt. Bearer of victory. But also translated into Saint Veronica who held a cloth to Jesus's face as as he carried his cross. The cloth of Veronica, *Volto Santo*, which supposedly carries on it an imprint of the face of Christ and has the power to quench thirst, cure the blind, even raise the dead.

* * *

Helen Noble, Helen Thomas. I imagine the Helen who endures so much in the twenty years of her difficult marriage. Helen, who for long spells is effectively a single parent to three children. Helen, whose optimism never quite gets ground down by the illness and cruelties of her husband and the poverty in which she exists. Helen, who loves her husband deeply. Helen who spends some of the happiest and some of the bleakest hours of her life in his company. Helen, the great letter writer. Helen, continuing her passion and talent for friendship, continuing to live a life that embraces the complexity and wonder of nature and hard domestic work. Helen, looking after her children and grandchildren. Helen like a window into the previous century. Helen, a widow to run across my own widow life. And you, Helen. A dedication.

* * *

Helen Noble met Edward Thomas when she was seventeen and he sixteen. Helen's father had been introduced to Edward by a Unitarian minister, and Edward, who had ambitions for a literary career, was taken under the family's wing. This was 1894. 'I and the Thomas boy are very slowly making our way,' Helen writes in a letter to her great and lifelong friend Janet Rogerson in 1896. There is something about the quality of a first missed encounter which she describes that threads its way through Edward's treatment of her throughout their marriage:

> He wrote and asked father if I might go out with him on one of his long walks. To my surprise he said I might. So I was in a great state of elation. But to my disappointment Edward never turned up for me. And when he came last night and was asked the reason, he said he had never dreamed I would be allowed to come.

In some ways it sounds like a poor excuse. Or the reasoning of a teenage boy who is frightened of what might happen should a girl and he take a walk. Or is it the response of someone not interested, trying to make his getaway? From Edward's point of view, as well as the perspective of the contemporary reader, the personal freedoms Helen details in her memoirs constantly run against our expectations of what might be seen as proper for a young middle-class educated woman at the time. Pregnant with Edward's child, for example, she does not feel the need to marry. She finds and rents a house in which she would like to live and employs a nurse of whom she is fond. Helen has a plan. And then the law of family removes her from this independence. Edward had taken up a History scholarship at Oxford in 1897. Full of propriety, he marries her in 1899, returns to complete his final year of studies, and Helen is persuaded to move instead into the house of her in-laws. Helen gives birth to their first child, Philip Merfyn Ashcroft on 15th January 1900. 'I and the Thomas boy are very slowly making our way'. The dynamics of their relationship set themselves up.

* * *

The pictures that exist of Helen tell several stories. The studio portraits work in contrast to the snaps of her, and show a very pretty young Edwardian, gazing into the middle distance; in the later photos, wearing her spectacles, her hair tied up in a way that suggests practicality rather than vanity, she is frequently pictured with children in her arms, or animals. There is something sensible and alive about her; perhaps a slightly-comical air; an ebullience born of a desire to please. There is also somewhere in her eyes a shyness, a doubting of herself which she is simultaneously trying to resist. When she describes herself in the first of her two best-selling memoirs of her life with Edward, *As it Was* (1926) and *World Without End* (1931) she does so in a way that feels self-deprecating but honest:

> *I was at that age plain, with a round healthy face and small nose, rather serious in expression, but not entirely unattractive. I had a lot of dark brown hair, which I wore parted in the middle with long plaits wound round my head … I was straight and tallish, and my own well-shaped and strong and – as I think of it now – really lovely body gave me intense delight. I loved being without clothes, and moving about naked, and I took pride in my health and strength.*

The picture in the archive that Edward carried with him to France sees her in almost full profile. There is something statuesque about this image, genial and ineradicable. And yet Helen is deeply conscious that – unlike Edward's friend Edna Clarke Hall – her looks are also something that Edward cannot idealise. Someone asks me if I'd have liked Helen. I pause. It is only when I hear her voice in a radio interview from 1967 – full of warmth, candour, self-knowledge, honesty, humour – that I am certain I would.

* * *

The sexual innocence of a generation of young men and women was signalled by the enormous success in 1918 of Marie Stopes'

Married Love: A Solution of the Sex Difficulties in Marriage. Helen's account of her friendship with Edward, their courtship, and the consummation of their relationship on Wimbledon Common, on Helen's twentieth-birthday, is written with passion and a shrewd attention to detail. *Soon*, she writes, *he came to a little glade in the copse, leafy and mossy and sunny, and putting me down knelt in front of me and undid my hair, but finding it fell over my face he picked a trial of white bryony and made a fillet of it to keep my hair back. Then keeping his eyes fixed so tenderly and seriously and passionately on mine...* The descriptions Helen gives of the slow sexual awakening of Edward are written with a tenderness she herself even refers to at one point as maternal. It was these accounts that, seemingly casting Edward in an unmanly light, most infuriated his great friend the American poet Robert Frost, but which also no doubt contributed to the popularity of the memoir when it was first published. Helen's accounts of her lovemaking are remarkably frank, especially when they speak about premarital relations, but unlike Marie Stopes she does not couch them in an ideology of exclusively marital bliss. Likewise in her account of the birth of her first baby, and her later calm advocacy of sex education for children, Helen appears able to sidestep convention; she is radical, remarkably forward-looking, practical, calm, sane.

* * *

The more I read and try to understand Helen, the more I start to assemble a picture of someone who lives through her instincts, who has a simple belief in right and wrong, good and bad. She is spontaneous, impulsive even; passionate; full of a belief in all that is good; she is capable of useful self-reflection. She is someone who believes in possibility; she is loyal, hardworking, patient, liberal, unconventional; she is fired by her readings of the Transcendentalists; she is Unitarian. I think about putting the word needy in that list. Her great-granddaughter describes her as 'quite difficult'. But both those words seem too much like a judgement and themselves beg questions: needy of what, difficult to whom? Helen wouldn't feel out of place in a novel or a poem by D.H. Lawrence; she reminds me, too, of Helen Wilcox in Forster's *Howards End*, of Tessa in *The Constant Nymph*. In a letter to Janet in August 1913, Helen is thoughtful about her own character:

> The fact is that nobody in this world but my sister knows me at all. I'm too simple and primitive in many things and too sensitive and morbid in other ways, and everyone even Edward makes the greatest mistakes about me. I'm like my mother a little, but more like Father, but it absolutely surprises me how people mistake my motives and reasons and point of view. I'm grateful for the bit of Mother in me, or else I had been crushed absolutely flat by now. I couldn't have gone on, had I not her wonderful power of recovery, and did I not love people all people so much that I could not hurt them if I could help it by showing how hurt I was. I often and often feel utterly lonely, and I am very lonely, for there is not one soul I know who really cares for me, and who tries to understand me, or thinks it worth the bother.

Don't come till the rain comes. Helen Thomas. Helen Noble, noble Helen Thomas.

*   *   *

At the same time as Helen tells her story in her memoirs, mediated always through the lens of her husband's needs and aspirations, there is still something of a mystery about her situation. Each time I come to think about her I seem to reach a dead end or impasse. She becomes what philosophers might call an aporia: a place where ideas cannot be resolved. I ask myself, what do I need to know by imagining Helen? The relationship with Edward – perhaps in the way we cannot really know anyone, or any marriage – seems closed to understanding from the outside because of the sharpness of its contradictions. But the relationship also starts to feel emblematic. It stands – and demands that I question – a dynamic of needs between men and women in a marriage that has writing and poetry at its heart. The relationship, I realise, becomes a place through which I try to understand what allows us to create, how we parent, how we mourn, and what it might mean to love.

*   *   *

Helen is not Edward's muse, but she is his constant. I think of other poets and their wives, some of them poets, some of them memoirists: Catherine Blake, Elizabeth Barrett Browning, Mary Shelley, Elinor Frost, Nadhezda Mandelstam, Caitlin Thomas, Elizabeth Hardwick, Sylvia Plath. Each name has a peculiar charge, holds a striking story. Helen seems both ill-treated and strong. She seems unwavering in her love. When she writes of trying to live with Edward, it is impossible not to feel huge sympathy. How would anyone behave in these circumstances? In a letter on the 29th June, 1904, she writes honestly, again to Janet her great confidante, of the reality of married life:

> Do these days seem good to you now I wonder, or does it seem foolishness that you and I, who are so far apart now, should have planned together these present days; should have talked of our lovers before I at least had one, or dared to hope for one; and our children when it seemed a light, pleasant thing to be mothers. And so it is pleasant, it is the most glorious thing in the world, but Oh the pain, and the care, and the responsibility. We did not think of that! How could we when we had no conception of any of those things.

Helen will do anything to make Edward happy – send him off to write while she cares for their three children alone, allow his friend Eleanor Farjeon, whom she suspects is in love with him, to spend time with them as a family. She struggles with domestic tasks, and the great doing and undoing of housework and gardening in which she also takes pride and some pleasure. But at the centre of their marriage is the strength of her commitment and love which continues after his death. It is hard not to ask what motivates this. *Poor Helen Thomas*. It is such an easy phrase. I think of her battling always Edward's absences and moods, her dedication to him having a writer's life, which in some part I expect she feels, through her early pregnancy, she has denied him. And yet. There is another line, that Helen, despite her unconventional views, is also a 'good' Edwardian wife who could not give up on her marriage. It is hard not to wonder what the options really were for Helen – or for any woman in a difficult marriage a hundred years ago.

* * *

My copy of *World Without End* – a birthday gift – is a first edition. It has a rust-coloured, slightly-battered cover, with an imprint of a windmill on the back. On the spine, below the title, only the initials HT, denote its author. Inside we encounter not Edward and Helen, but David and Jenny. One passage stands out for me, when Jenny talks of David's return at the end of a day when he has been out looking for work. *'I could do nothing,'* she writes,

> *for if I said one word which would betray that I knew what*
> *he had endured and was enduring, his anger and despair*
> *and weariness would break out in angry and bitter words*
> *which would freeze my heart and afterwards freeze his for*
> *having uttered them. … sometimes when his spirit had*
> *been more than usually affected by the too great strain that*
> *circumstances put upon it, the cloud did not pass, and my*
> *chatter ran dry in the arid silence. After a ghastly hour or*
> *two with the supper still uneaten on the kitchen table he*
> *would say, 'Go to bed, I'm not coming' and I would know*

that he would sit up all night, and in the morning would be
deeper in despair than ever. I did not sleep on these nights
but took my baby into bed with me, and in suckling him and
holding him close, hope and comfort came to me again.

This image of Helen bringing her child to her breast where
perhaps she also wished her husband might have been, seeking the warmth of a body which also needs her, is a devastating
image. And I wonder, as she sat and wrote, exactly what she felt
as she held her love and her despair so close.

* * *

I imagine Edward, preoccupied, suffering what his friend, the
analyst-in-training, Godwin Baynes describes as an 'erotic
complex'. Edward, desperate, isolated, unfulfilled. Edward,
charming, gentle, shy, full of fun. Edward, singing Welsh folk
songs; naming the birds and the plants, walking with a great
lolopping stride. Edward, playing with verve and energy with
his children, letting them clamber over him, throwing them up
on his shoulders. Edward, taking his son Merfyn on long bike
rides. Edward, out of love, exhausted, trapped. Edward, writing
compulsively because he cannot face the pain within himself.
Edward, brilliant at projecting the pain he cannot bear onto
Helen more than any other. Edward, desperate to become the
kind of writer he himself would praise. Edward Thomas, father,
husband: poet Edward Eastaway.

Helen, doing all she can to support her husband. Helen, clumsy, eager, cheerful, perhaps overbearing. Helen, putting all her energies into housekeeping, and all her creativity into being a good mother and wife. Helen, sociable, exhausted, isolated, frightened. The same Helen who can match Edward's thirty mile walks; who attended a lecture by Oscar Wilde, who visited her school; who at eighteen handled the manuscripts of Blake's *Songs of Innocence* in the British Library; who made a trip to the Keats House in Hampstead to sit under the mulberry tree where Keats wrote 'Ode to a Nightingale'; who, owing to a strong interest in the pre-Raphaelites, called one afternoon on William Morris. Helen, aching for the companionship and joy of her relationship with Edward to be renewed. Helen, selfless, wanting only the best for her husband, defying convention, trying not to 'own' Edward.

Helen, so much in love with her husband, that her body can hardly contain the feelings of pleasure and pain their relationship brings her. Helen, writing in 1910: 'What times we've had! What rapture, what despair, and always our love absolutely undisturbed, like a great beautiful placid bird, spreading its wings over us.' Helen, the martyr. Helen, relieved to have another adult in the house when Eleanor visits, to defend against Edward's harms and her great loneliness, to help her with the children. *A bowl of white violets*. Helen, knowing that actually having Edward out of the house was the only way to prevent the pain and pervasion of his moods, his illness. Helen, when she hears that Edward will return from France for Christmas in 1916, buying herself a beautiful red dress.

Edward, irresponsibly involved in a passionate friendship with a teenage girl who is in his care. Helen, who can warn Edward to be careful in this situation; Edward, who is found out by the girl's family, and returns home to Helen saying that a girl of the earth is worth more than any mermaid. Helen, clear-eyed, courageous, enduring, resigned when she writes that:

> *Edward must work out his own salvation in his own way. And his way was my way. Life for him would always be painful, but at least he had the country which meant so much to him, and the freedom within the limits his poverty imposed — and with his simple tastes and needs this was not too obvious, the circumstances of his life were what he had chosen, and I would not encourage him to consider changing them. All I could do now was to try to convey my own faith in him and in his work, and my own freedom from sadness and anxiety.*

Edward, self-lacerating, self-damning, egotistical, appalled at himself in the face of Helen's goodness. The man who can chillingly write in 1916 that he has lost the capacity to love. All the Helens and Edwards of twenty years of marriage. How can we measure her pain against his?

* * *

What other lives do I imagine for them, then, or now? In one of many alternative universes Helen is divorced, living as a single mother; Edward is a responsible but distant father, living with another woman whom he loves. Here's Helen again, feeling slightly out of her depth, but nevertheless falling in with a set of poets and writers and moving to Paris in the 1920s. Or maybe there's an Edward who decides not to go to war, is taken up by a rich patron, and spends every day writing poems; Eleanor types them up for him, and devotes herself to his happiness. Or let me look again. Here are Helen and Edward and Eleanor living in a *ménage à trois*. Here are Eleanor and Helen living together, bringing up Edward's children, Edward pursuing a string of young women to whom he writes his poems. Here's Edward seeking a psychoanalytic cure with Jung; an Edward, well enough to be able to deal with the collapse of a marriage and to hold out hope for something better. Here is Helen, wary of the class assumptions of Bloomsbury, but nevertheless at home with their sexual frankness. Here is Helen, the artist's model, or Helen with her love of theatre, writing plays. Or, if I think again, here now is Edward returning from the war to find his poems have made him an established and respected poet; Edward avoiding divorcing Helen because he cannot bear the lack of respectability this brings. Edward, finding happiness in his writing, at last. Or now, an Edward, wounded or shell-shocked, even less able to exist within the family....

Here's Helen, instead, with Eleanor sleeping beside her to comfort her during the first bewildering weeks after Edward's death. Here's Helen, who can bear no more, now that her children are old enough to sustain themselves, falling to pieces, break-ing down, writing her books as a way to recover, slowly coming to terms with the nature of her marriage and her self and her loss. Who could she have become? It's a question we can ask of all our unfolding lives.

* * *

On impulse I decide to visit the Edward Thomas Archive at the University of Cardiff, which I visit with my thirteen year old daughter. We are shown into a glass-edged room. On the table are a set of cardboard boxes and inside, wrapped in paper and tied with strips of linen ribbons, objects from the couple's lives. Here is a pair of candlesticks which must surely be the candlesticks Helen bought for Edward's Oxford rooms; a letter Helen has written and enclosed in the copy of a Richard Jeffries book they loved, and which contains Edward's pencil markings, underlinings. Here is a quilt that Helen has made in the 1940s, as brilliant and gaudy as a psychedelic honeycomb. As I tentatively unwrap each bundle, I suddenly find I have opened a box that contains Edward's possessions sent home from France, after his death. I feel like I have secretly stumbled on a tomb, and here are the grave goods. I do not know how to look at these objects without feeling I am committing an act of trespass. Here is a set of pipes with tobacco in that is a hundred years old; a handkerchief in red and white with the initials ET inked in the corner; here is Edward's round silver tobacco tin which I hold in my hands like I am about the take communion. Here is Edward's wallet, still containing calling cards, scribbled with engagements. Here is a photograph of Helen, warped in a way that suggests it might have been the photograph found on Edward's body, riddled with the physical power of an

Helen Thomas

explosion's blast. I am not sure what the power and charge is of these objects, or the quality of intimacy I share in handling them. Flakes of tobacco stick to my hands, crumble onto the library table; also in the box are sachets of lavender. I raise them to my nose and inhale. Tears run down my face. The smell of the past. The weight.

* * *

Widowhood is a strange state that still positions a woman within the fidelity of her marriage vows, even though her husband is no longer there. In a recent study of working-class widows of the Great War, Angela Smith has shown how the young widow was vulnerable to accusations of 'cohabitation, prostitution, child-neglect and drunkenness'; her pension, the first non-means tested, non-contributory allowance to be directed to British women, also depended on the widow's ability to show herself a 'fit' mother. As Smith also points out, the word widow is one of the few words which is modified to apply for a male equivalent, rather than the other way around. Helen was a widow for fifty years, though perhaps she might not have described herself like that. I'm curious about the lives of other widows whose husbands were lost in the war. Helen, we are told, refused to wear black after Edward's death, unlike the two other widows in the village where she and Myfanwy lived. I think of the widows in India who committed suttee, of the town south east of Delhi, Vrindavan, a site of pilgrimage which celebrates the love of Krishna and Radha, and is now home to as many as six thousand widows. I think about the marital status forms I have filled in myself which still ask you: single, married, divorced, widow, widower. *Widow / widower. Author / authoress.*

* * *

My great-grandfather, James Douglas, fought in the war, surviving doubtless though sheer good luck, only to suffer the effects of the gas he inhaled, and to meet, ten years later, his own premature, but civilian death. Family memory is hazy. Was this mustard gas? Tear gas? Can I imagine the fear the soldiers felt when faced with chemical clouds? Or when their eyes streamed and their skin blistered? After the war, there were frequent trips to the coast for my grandmother and her parents — to Morecambe and Fleetwood — in the hope that the sea air would help with James' respiratory problems. Like Edward, James would have joined up voluntarily as an older man. On the census form his occupation is listed as barman. His parents were wheelwrights. Doubtless his reasons for joining up were not easily explained. Perhaps, like Edward, he joined up for a complex mixture of emotional and economic reasons. In the only photograph I have of James, taken in a photographer's studio on Church Street in central Liverpool, he is wearing his soldier's uniform. Across his body he wears what I suppose is a leather ammunition strap. He is sitting in a wooden chair, which has elaborately-carved Chinese dragons as armrests. I see my uncle's face in him, as well as my grandmother's, and my own, a glimmer of my son's. There is something in his eyes of the hunted, the haunted. Is it a family or a generation's trait?

The Parisian Studios 27 Church St Liverpool

James Douglas

* * *

As always the past rises up to meet us; riddles its way through our present and future, wobbles, overlaps, runs away. On February 12th, 1915, did my eight-year-old grandmother, Elizabeth, catch a glimpse of a woman and a seventeen-year-old boy stepping off a London train at Lime Street en route to the liner bound for America, newly-moored at the dock? Perhaps Helen Thomas, in a long and unfashionable coat, approached my great-grandmother, and her daughter, as she hurried to meet the Frosts, for directions. My great-grandmother, enjoying a pleasant walk in the sunshine in the company of this woman and her teenage son, offers to take them to the café where they will meet the Frosts. They arrive early, and over a cup of tea Merfyn and Elizabeth look at each other, suddenly, painfully self-aware. Merfyn is wondering what a life in America will mean for him, away from his family and the difficult relationship he has with his father. Lily, as Elizabeth now prefers to be called, is doe-eyed, sociable. Her own father is away at war, and she is keen to impress. She tells Merfyn in her Liverpool accent which is tinged also with the rhythms and vowel sounds of her Scottish and her Irish relatives, how she had nearly died earlier that year of rheumatic fever. Every morning she would swim thirty or forty lengths of the newly-built swimming pool. Swimming is her passion. But when she got sick she had to practice lying as still as possible. 'Lie still', the doctors murmured, 'or your heart might stop.' With great pride she brings out from her pocket a rosary her father had found on the body of dead French soldier. She is not a Catholic, though one day she will toy with a conversion.

Every night she prays, saying the Lord's Prayer, kneeling at the end of her bed. Merfyn listens, though his mind is elsewhere. Already he is missing the colours of the countryside he has left. The city is dirty and the buildings close down the sky. He boasts a little of the American poet with whom he is to make his enormous journey. But Lily isn't sure why anyone would leave their family. And what anyway, has poetry to do with anything? As they walk, Merfyn whistles. And Helen looks at her son and remembers undressing on Wimbledon Common when she was not much older than he is now. And with a sweet stabbing pang she remembers the first time Edward himself undressed and came to her. *He picked a little bunch of flowers in the grass, white clover, yellow bedstraw and milkwort...* But perhaps, in the steam and the blur of the engines and the grime and the dirt of the city, with the melancholy sound of the newspaper seller crying *Echo* on the corner of the street, the two mothers, Helen and my great-grandmother, walk past each other without a thought; and none of this happened at all.

* * *

Greenfinches settle in the tree outside my kitchen window. I am learning the names of birds. The world becomes alive in the naming of it. Sometimes the world can feel too noisy, too bright. A pair of collared turtle doves coo. Yet I look out, and listen, because once you have started to see and hear the world in all its detail, you can't turn back. Now I have no choice. I think of Helen, who has learned to name the world and see it through Edward's eyes. I take my own pleasure in Helen's unbroken joy when she still finds time to walk with her husband; and I laugh outloud when I read in her memoir that she was never cured of walking out of synch, one step ahead of her husband.

* * *

One in ten of men under forty-five died during the war. This is still a startling fact. While thinking about Helen and Edward I reread Rebecca West's *The Return of the Soldier* which, published in 1918, gives a brilliant account of one man's return from battle with shell shock. The soldier has no memory of the beautiful but emotionally cold woman he has married, but instead wants only to return to the arms of a now middle-aged and poverty-worn woman who was his first love. It must have been a question Helen asked herself a thousand times. What if Edward had not gone to war? Or, what if Edward had come back?

* * *

Lily Thomas, no relative to Edward, but my own grandmother, is sitting in a dark back room with her father. The war is over. It is many months since he has returned to them. Ordinary life begins again. Except nothing is ordinary and everything is changed. A loving daughter, Lily pushes her hair behind her ears, rests her head on her father's lap. At twenty she is still Lily Douglas. Not long after her father has died she will lose her fiancé, Alec, to tuberculosis. But right now, she doesn't know this; nor does she know how one day she will talk to her own granddaughter about how it felt to love someone who was dangerously ill. 'They said we could hold hands, but we were no longer allowed to kiss', is what I remember she said to me. But what does she say to her father, in the half-light as he smokes, coughs, now, a hundred years ago? On the mantelshelf there is a photograph. Here is Lily at seventeen, posing for a camera wearing her father's own unfathomable expression. She looks out at me, wearing a gypsy dress.

* * *

The most moving item in the boxes I open at the archive in Cardiff is a little notebook into which Helen has inscribed two of Edward's poems and two letters written to Edward after his death between April 9th and June 17th, 1917. Given that she had written to Edward for over half of her life, it isn't surprising that she would wish to continue the conversation. In these letters she writes of the coming Spring:

> Such a Spring of flowers and birds and colour and peace and sound after all that terrible winter. All the flowers came out together, except the May which was very late. We found it once on May Day do you remember! And lying in the orchard under the very old apple trees heavy with blossom and full of bees I listened to the nightingale and the cuckoo and touched the moist green grass and lay listening and looking and hearing and touching and filling my soul with it and gather it all into myself as I have gathered you in my arms beloved. Because it is you I feel in it all, and we are very close all the time and I am

Lily Thomas

almost content sweet heart that it should be so.

If Winter comes, can Spring be far behind? The poems Helen picks to copy out are 'March' and 'November'. They are two of Edward's earliest poems. 'I found spring all along the road,' writes Edward in 1913 in the final lines of his remarkable account of a journey from London to the Quantocks, *In Pursuit of Spring*. Winter and Spring are as central to Helen's under-standing of Edward's fluctuating moods, as they are to his own. Spring is part of a natural cycle of renewal and rebirth which Helen places at the centre of her mourning: remembering, but also looking forward in a dialogue with hope.

* * *

Love is patient and kind; love does not envy or boast; it is not arrogant or rude. It does not insist on its own way; it is not irritable or resentful; it does not rejoice at wrongdoing, but rejoices with the truth. Love bears all things, believes all things, hopes all things, endures all things. Love never ends. (Corinthians). *Love isn't something natural. Rather it requires discipline, concentration, patience, faith, and the overcoming of narcissism. It isn't a feeling, it is a practice.* (Eric Fromm)

* * *

Not having seen Edward's lifeless but undamaged body, and with no English grave to visit, I imagine it was hard for a long time for Helen to realise properly that Edward had gone. 'The dead are always with us', writes the poet Alice Oswald, thinking of the women who mourn in her great poem of the devastations of war, *Memorial*. The dead are always with us, I think. But also, and in obvious and important ways, they are not. Given that Edward was absent for so many long stretches of Helen's life, there must have been days when Edward did not seem dead at all, and life returned to an ordinariness, gathering itself up into its routines. When Edward was walking, Helen often did not know where he was. She does not know when he is dead where he is either. *Coo-ee*, call the lovers, negotiating and repeating the moments when they are not together as if in some Freudian 'fort-da' game.

* * *

I think about the ways in which grief is held in the body: anniversaries of weddings, birthdays, consummations. All fill the body's rhythms, their significance rising and falling in unexpected ways. To mourn, says Freud, the ego must slowly and painfully withdraw its attachment from the beloved object. Our lost ones must be fully internalized for the work of mourning to be complete. In time, grief becomes a co-existent, harmonious, in that it has become part of a range of feeling. In a strange, slow, invisible act of decomposition the beloved becomes more alive, less an absence or a person located in the past outside your body, but more a part of the internal sense of yourself, integrated not running counter or against (as I imagine something unresolved in ourselves might: a haunting, a ghost), in a kind of continuous and reassuring presence.

When I try to describe my own experience of mourning I find that healing or recovery – or whatever words we have to mark the temporal movement away from a loved one's death – is not linear. Mourning demands an engagement with the present and the past as well as the future, and grief has the ability to permeate and overwrite all parts of your daily experience. As well as its very simple manifestation in physical pain, sometimes the grief of mourning is not a feeling at all, but something that you are always moving away from as well as moving towards; it is simply an orientation. Sometimes it becomes an idiom you can only measure other experiences against. The relationship between physical and mental pain is always a surprising one. What is also shocking, though, is the intense way in which grief has the capacity to make the sweet sweeter. Life can be more intense, more immediate, more full, more obviously precious.

* * *

Coo-ee call the lovers. Cooooooooooo-ee. In the photographs of Edward as a solider, crop-haired and gaunt, sporting a moustache, he has lost his good looks. He is preparing for death. But Helen describes him being happier than he had been for many years. His poems, over one hundred and forty of them, seem now to write themselves, pour out. *Don't come till the rain comes. I have a superstitious feeling that with the rain good will come all round. This drought is unnatural and unkind, though I do love the sun and the blue sky of it. But the rain and the sweet smell of wet earth would bring relief to the soul of me.*

Edward Thomas' first poem can be dated to December 3rd, 1914, his last to the 13th January, 1917. He died on April 8th 1917. It is almost as if he is picking up in the world his inner emotional thread as the narrative of war and his own likely death run concurrently with his own depressive tendency, his wavering but constant desire for self-annihilation.

* * *

Edward had met the American poet Robert Frost in 1914, and it was arranged that their two families would spend the coming summer together. Helen's account of her journey to meet her husband and the Frost family in Ledbury on the 28th July, the day when war broke out, is vivid in its evocation of the panic and suspicion their arrival caused. What was to be made of a woman arriving at the station at midnight with two of her children and a Russian boy from Bedales school who was staying with them for the holidays?

It is an unnaturally hot July when I first make a trip to the house the Frosts rented, 'Little Iddens', and stand at the gate of a field to look across to the farm where Edward and Helen stayed. Between the two houses is an oak tree. Beyond are apple orchards. The walk between the two houses might have taken half an hour. With his long gait it would have taken Edward less. When I come here again with the artist Charlotte Hodes we walk slowly across the fields. We do not know each other very well, but there is no shortage of conversation. I love the way the length of the grass pulls our feet into the depths of the field. From time to time as we walk, we stop, looking forwards, looking back, taking our measure of what we can see. I am very taken with the oak tree which lies equidistant between the two houses. Its shadows are as dark and solid as it is. Did Helen send the children out into the fields with bread and cheese to picnic here? Or did she sit here herself, alive to the buzz and hum and birdsong of the fields? As we stand, at the far edge of the field, a hare quivers, watching us.

* * *

R. George Thomas' magnificently researched and measured biography of Edward Thomas quotes a letter in which Eleanor Farjeon writes that for Edward 'to be able to hurt a woman as he did Helen, and not to break her, to be so sure she was strong enough to bear anything from him, was the most wonderful thing of all.' Eleanor continues: 'I couldn't have borne it myself without breaking, and often couldn't for her.' It is unclear here whether what is most wonderful is Edward's belief in Helen's resilience, or Helen's actual capacity to endure the mental pain her inflicts on her. The muddle of Eleanor's sentence bears testimony, surely, to Eleanor's own confusion about how to read the marriage. Endurance, I think, by its very nature, cannot endure forever.

* * *

As well as dealing with her grief, sorting out her own financial situation with no obvious source of income apart from a widow's pension, must not have been easy for Helen. The War Widow's Pension in 1917 would have paid her £26 pounds a year. In 2013 the payments for war widows are equally small, and hover around the £7000 a year mark. In 1917 there would have been payment for dependents under fourteen, and provision for occasional payments. In the National Archives, Kew, you can trawl through a random selection of the applications widows made in order to be eligible for these funds. The forms ask for the details of date and place of the injury or death of a spouse. And as Helen enters into the complicated relationship between widow and state, reduces her grief to words on a form, the relationship between Helen and Edward, even in death, is reconfigured in financial terms. I think of lines from an early poem by Denise Riley, 'Affections Must Not', when she describes so wonderfully 'the fine steely wires that run to and fro between love and economics'.

* * *

At the same time as I imagine Helen, a woman grieving a hundred years ago, I also try to imagine a nation which collectively must learn the stabs and anomalies, and strange internal time-travelling of grief. It is hard to evaluate the distress of the widows, mothers, sisters, of the soldiers whose bodies were not returned to England. Or to understand the particular kind of private mourning that must have been undergone in the face of national and collective grief. The death of young men must have seemed unnatural as well as rationalised through the narratives of warfare. It is hard to put myself in the mindset of widows who later, crossing a road, were reminded through public memorials, of their own private grief, each death with its own invisible story, each with its own unknowable pain. The disjuncture between private and public mourning becomes highlighted at every turn. Death makes a pariah of those who are left behind. Death carries with it silence. Awkwardness. Those who are not grieving, are at a loss, with a lack of words to say. At exactly the same time the ideology of war overwrites with generalities. The newly worn identity of 'war widow' becomes a new part of the self. I imagine at times this helps, and that at other times it makes everything feel much worse.

* * *

As Helen drew on all her inner resources to continue to care for her children, she was also deeply engaged in the bittersweet process of publication of Edward's poems, with volumes appearing first in 1917, then in 1918, and followed in 1920 by his *Collected Poems*. Since the publication of those first books, Edward Thomas' poems have never been out of print. I wonder if at the time Helen thought of the love she shared with Edward of Shelley's poems, and thought then of Mary Shelley, and her valiant efforts to keep her own husband's poetic reputation alive.

Doubtless writing her memoirs not only added to the burgeoning reputation of Edward's writing, but performed a function in Helen's own grieving process as her own mental health declined. One accusation that seems to be thrown at the memoirs is that Helen is in some way deluded; that the accounts are over-romanticised. In fact, Helen is nothing but perceptive about her relationship with Edward. It is not just a strength of the memoirs, but is perhaps the key to her daily ability to withstand all the difficulties the relationship holds for her. Confiding again to her friend Janet in a letter on the 9th January, 1908, Helen writes:

> I would have liked after all this vain striving to have felt that I had had a finger in the pie. He is my whole life, my love in whose existence I exist and yet I can do so little, so very little for him. I know that a lot of the spirit in me is gone, and I had been a far better, wiser, more helpful wife if I had not let him mould me as he liked. One can love too well. To see him happy is what I want, and he has said it was impossible. Not that I believed him, but the thing was to find the key to the door of the empty chamber where happiness ought to live. And I believe it has been found; and if he gets health the door will be kept always open now.

To wish for the happiness of another as the only way to find happiness for yourself seems a terrible burden. But as much as she wishes the best for Edward, Helen is aware that she must also struggle to hold on to her own sense of self, and keep her independence. *Spring could do nothing to make me sad.* I think about this for a long time, this, and the nature of a need to idealise poetry, to idealise the living and the dead.

* * *

2, Yew Tree Cottage, Steep, stands at the end of a long alley flanked with elderberries. It was here that Helen and Edward lived with their three children and occasional summer board-ers from Bedales school, between 1913 and 1916, after their move from a large and imposing house on the nearby hills. When I visit with Emma Harding, who is producing a radio programme we are making about Helen, we miss the sharp turning up to the cottage. It is raining, and although it is only set about a hundred yards back from the road, the cottage feels a long way from the main road through the village. The yew tree that gave it its name has recently been cut down, but has started to sprout shoots. The cottage itself is semi-detached, and its other half is a groomed, twenty-first century dwelling, freshly-painted, its lawn neatly mown. But the poet's half might not have changed in the last sixty or even a hundred years, co-existing with its immaculate counterpart in what might be a separate pocket of time. Surrounded by garden on three sides, with its higgledy-piggledy vegetable and flower patches, abandoned watering cans and seed pots, there is something hugely improvised and alive about the house; it has its original windows and the frames and the guttering are painted a bril-liant grass green. There is something about its situation, too, which opens you up immediately to trees and fields and sky. Yet Helen describes how Edward always longed for the height of the hills behind the house, where he would walk to the rented outbuilding where he wrote.

It is here, then, that many of Thomas' poems might have been conceived. It is here in the tiny front room with its open fireplace that according to R. George Thomas, Edward read his poems aloud to Helen. There is a sense of calm and magic about the cottage, and I wonder if Helen and Edward felt that too. It is easy to romanticise in retrospect. I wonder were they warm. How did they wash themselves and their clothes, five people jostling in this tiny space? There is a photograph of Edward with Myfanwy and the young son of a neighbour outside the cottage which must have been taken in around 1913. Myfanwy, round-faced, cherubic, as shortsighted as her mother, looks at the camera with assurance and great presence. Edward, in tie and sweater, has his face turned slightly away.

Outside the front door is the 'Old Man' plant that Helen had grown from a cutting and which Edward famously writes about in his poem of the same name. I rub the leaves between my fingers, and take in the wood and lemon smell. As we stand there in the cold drizzle of a February morning, talking with the current inhabitant, and I read Edward's poems aloud for our recording, I see nearby a great spotted woodpecker and take delight in the endless moment of its perch and drum on the side of a tree.

* * *

'And you, Helen'. What now can I make of Edward's only poem directed to his wife? Between March 29th and April 9th,

1916 Edward wrote a series of poems for his family, which he referred to collectively as his 'household' poems and which he originally intended to be published together in a separate book. The sequence, with its wonderful developing idiom, works as a complex meditation on the relationship between father and family, family and nation, husband and wife, addressing the very nature of familial inheritance and bequest.

While the first two poems begin with the conditional 'if', all four poems are littered with 'shoulds' and 'woulds', and hover somewhere between what J.L. Austin might call a 'performative utterance' (something which produces the reality of what it is naming in the act of naming) and, because they exist in the realm of the hypothetical, a more fantasy-driven wish-fulfillment. Thomas' first two 'gifts' to his children are full of references to land and ownership. In the first of the sequence we find the repeating words 'rich', 'rent', 'rent', 'rich'; in the second we find the words 'own', 'giving or letting', 'let', 'pay', 'rent'. In the later two poems we find this repeating vocabulary of economics: 'richer', 'leave', 'wanting'; in the poem to Helen we find the words 'store' and 'treasure-house'.

During this time Thomas was enlisted in the Artists' Rifles and working at Hare Hall Camp in Romford where he was in March promoted to Corporal. While financial anxieties must have been a constant undercurrent in Edward's consciousness, the geographical nature of the poems is also underpinned by his new occupation as a map-reading instructor. In 'If I were to own' Merfyn is putatively 'given' a list of places in the

Essex countryside: 'Skreens, Gooshays, and Cockerells / Shel-
low, Rochetts, Bandish, and Pickerells / Martins, Lambkins,
and Lillyputs'. But in the context of the poem they stop being
places, and instead become sounds, things in themselves, of
which the poem itself has taken ownership.

* * *

Edward's poem to Helen stands apart in composition dates
from the three slightly earlier poems, though thematically has
more in common with the third poem, to Myfanwy. Helen is the
only family member to be directly named in this set of poems,
and it is the only poem to make a direct address. In the other
poems the children are referred to in terms of their gender and
order in the family. 'And you, Helen', however, writes Helen
into its fabric by direct invocation. Yet, this poem is not *to* Helen or
for Helen. It holds no dedication. Like the poem to his then six
year old daughter, to whom, Lear-like, Edward says he will give
nothing, the poem echoes God's question to Solomon, 'What
Shall I give you?' in *Kings* 3, 5, and carries with the intertextual
echo all the imperious tone of the divine speaking to the hu-
man. What shall I give you, asks a divine Edward placing Helen
in the role of a Solomon, who asks for wisdom.

> I would give you back to yourself,
>
> And power to discriminate
>
> What you want and want it not too late,
>
> Many fair days free from care

And heart to enjoy both foul and fair.

And myself, too, if I could find

Where it lay hidden and it proved kind.

The poem demands an answer (this doesn't in this context feel so much a rhetorical question any more) and at the same time takes away the ability to answer with its answer. The gift that is given is something which at the same time its giver is taking away. At some level, then, the poem works as implicit criticism. You are old, you are short sighted, you are indiscriminate, it seems to say. I will give you a clear eye like mine; you are, at least at an intertextual level, not very clever, because what you need to answer this question, what you will ask for, is wisdom. Essentially then, 'And you, Helen' is a poem built on the powerlessness and inadequacies of its addressee. The 'you' to whom the wish of the poem is being given is to be given back to herself; but the self who gives, paradoxically, even though he has speech and the power to give, is proffered, and then at the end of the poem taken away. There is no gift to be given if there is no giver. Perhaps the poem, too, is an answer to Helen's increasing anxieties about the unnamed addressee of other of Edward's poems that speak on the one hand of the inability to love, or of desire that is apparently located elsewhere. Does Edward's poem, a gift that declares it probably has nothing to give, situate the poem itself as a substitution for giving? I have nothing to give you, I am myself nothing, but at least I have written a poem?

'And you, Helen' also carries more complex associations and literary echoes than its biblical ones. 'Ask nothing more of me, sweet / All I can give you, I give', writes Swinburne in 'The Oblation' before arguing 'I that have love and no more / give you but love of you, sweet.' Thomas knew Swinburne's poem well and had published a critical book on him in 1912. Swinburne's poem suggests that if the poet does not love the beloved to her to her satisfaction, it is because she herself is somehow not enough. This is a clever move in the rhetoric of love, and acts as a kind of mirror to Thomas' suggestion that if he had a self he would give Helen back herself. The word oblation, means literally in Greek 'offering'; we are much more familiar, of course, with the idea of a poem including a dedication, the etymology of which is not about offering something but of making new. As Thomas remembers Swinburne he is also invoking the last lines of Walt Whitman's 'Song of the Open Road', again a poem Thomas knew well:

> I give you my love more precious than money,
>
> I give you myself before preaching and law;
>
> Will you give me yourself? Will you come travel with me?
>
> Shall we stick by each other as long as we live?

But unlike Whitman's poem of open-ness and the receptiveness of the world to self, Thomas' poem is about psychic destitution. *And it proved kind*. There is a genius to Thomas' use of that word which simultaneously evokes the natural order: kinship, kindness. A phrase slips into my consciousness: payment in kind.

* * *

For the French theorist Marcel Mauss, in his seminal study of giving, *The Gift*, there is something invested in the act of giving that can never sidestep an implicit demand of reciprocation. To give one must also, almost magically, give a part of oneself. Drawing on Mauss's work, the philosopher Derrida suggests that the true gift is always an impossibility. For Derrida, even the act of saying 'thank you' for a gift suggests a debt has been paid. The only gift we can ever truly receive is one we do not know we have been given.

In interview in 1967, Helen remarks how when he was leaving the house one day Edward handed her the 'And you, Helen' poem saying, 'Read this when I have gone'. As I imagine Edward walking away and Helen holding the poem, wondering what she can make of it, the poem starts to stand for something very painful that occurs between them. As an ungiving gift, the poem's own unique impossibility does not replicate Derrida's sense that true altruism cannot ever exist, but rather takes comfort, compensates the poetic self in itself, in its attempt at giving. Unlike the other family poems which situate their gifts in the land and the natural world, and which are written so that the 'I' of the poem gives to a third person, keeping things open-ended and possible, the poem to Helen establishes a perpetual loop between an 'I' and a 'you' whose condition of existence depends entirely on each other. The only external things given are general and not particular, and are shrunk into a single line: 'Lands, waters, flowers, wine'. The more I read the poem – Helen is standing there reading it, Edward is walking away – the more I get a measure of its sleight of hand at posing as a gift that is no gift. And perhaps what hurts me as a reader most is the fact that it dramatises brilliantly a complexity of relations, which is also, as I imagine, part of the very real and painful *impasse* that becomes a hallmark of the Thomas marriage.

* * *

A letter from Edward to Myfanwy, written in 1916, when she was six, has obviously been written slowly and neatly. It talks chattily of a lost baby tooth as well as Edward's desire to write, if he can only find a table. Like so much that passes between Helen and Edward when death hovers over them, it is heartbreaking. It ends: Goodbye. Daddy.

* * *

All and always yours, Edwy. Coo-ee call the lovers. A message on my answer phone: I'm Helen and Edward's granddaughter, Myfanwy's daughter. Coo-ee back down the past. *All I can give you I give.*

* * *

Just as I am curious about the way in which Helen dealt with her life with Edward, I am equally fascinated by the life she went

Helen, with one of her grandchildren.

on to lead. In a late letter to the now estranged Frost, filling him in on the last thirty years of her life, she writes of 'a struggling often despairing time'. Still, she continues, 'somehow or other I have come through'. In another letter I chance on in the Cardiff archive, Rosemary, Myfanwy's daughter, describes the house where Helen lived for twenty years at Starwell, near Chippenham, Wiltshire, as primitive: 'no electricity, earth closet outside and water from a pump by the back door – no drains'. It was here that Helen continued to look after daughters, and grandchildren.

It is astonishing, the sense of resilience in the face of continuing tragedy that the family shows: Helen, living to see her son die; Bronwen, their eldest daughter, a young widow and mother, whose first husband died of a brain tumour, surviving two further husbands; Myfanwy, who has a child with Henry Williamson, author of *Tarka the Otter*, doing so as a single mother (Williamson, a man like her father in so many ways, with his love of nature and his difficult temperament, also fought in the Great War, returning home traumatised). And yet, Helen's innate optimism remains: 'I & my two girls are so close to each other and their children that when I am with them I think what a fortunate rich woman I am' writes Helen. *I would give you back to yourself.*

* * *

Five days before Edward dies, Helen writes to Janet: 'I think he is wonderful doing his soldier's work... but Oh, tho' my soul is perfectly content, my poor old body does want him.'

* * *

A newsletter for the Edward Thomas Fellowship, dated 1988, notes that Helen and Edward's first great granddaughter has her birthday on March 4th.

The rain and the sweet smell of the wet earth. Her name is Helen.

NOTES

The phrase 'wings of glass' used in the poem quotes Sylvia Plath's poem 'Stings'

Unless otherwise indicated sections from Helen Thomas' memoirs *As it Was* and *World Without End* are quoted, without footnote, in italics in the text.

'If Winter comes, can Spring be far behind?' is the last line of Shelley's 'Ode to the West Wind'

WORKS CITED AND CONSULTED

Roland Barthes, *A Lover's Discourse: Fragments* (London: Vintage, 2002).

Jacques Derrida, *The Gift of Death*, translated by David Wills (Chicago and London: University of Chicago Press, 1995).

_____, *The Work of Mourning*, ed. Pascale-Anne Brault and Michael Naas (Chicago and London: University of Chicago Press, 2003).

Eleanor Farjeon, with a foreword by P.J. Kavanagh, and an introduction and editing of revised edition by Anne Harvey, *Edward Thomas: The Last Four Years* (London: Faber, 2010).

Sigmund Freud, *On Murder, Mourning and Melancholia*, translated by Shaun Whiteside, with an introduction by Maud Ellmann (London: Penguin, 2005).

Eric Fromm, *The Art of Loving* (London:Thorsons, 2010).

Matthew Hollis, *Now All Roads Lead to France: The Last Years of Edward Thomas* (London: Faber, 2011).

Sagar Keith, ed., *D.H.Lawrence: Selected Poetry* (London: Penguin, revised edition, 1975).

Edna Longley, *Poetry in the Wars* (Newcastle: Bloodaxe, 1986).

_____, ed., *The Annotated Collected Poems* (Tarset: Bloodaxe, 2008).

Marcel Mauss, *The Gift: Forms and Functions of Exchange in Archaic Societies*, trans. W.D. Halls, with a foreword by Mary Douglas (London: Routledge, 2001).

Sharon Ouditt, *Fighting Forces, Writing Women: Identity and Ideology in the First World War* (London: Routledge, 1994).

Angela Smith, *Discourses Surrounding British Widows of the First World War* (London: Bloomsbury, 2013).

Stan Smith, *Edward Thomas* (London: Faber and Faber, 1986).

Matthew Spencer, ed, with foreword by Michael Hofmann and afterword by Christopher Ricks, *Elected Friends: Robert Frost and Edward Thomas To One Another* (New York: Other Press, 2003).

Sean Street, *The Dymock Poets* (Bridgend: Seren, 1994).

Edward Thomas, with an introduction by Glen Cavaliero, *The Happy-Go-Lucky Morgans* (Woodbridge, The Boydell Press, 1983).

Helen Thomas, *Time and Again: Memoirs and Letters* (Manchester: Carcanet, 1978).

Helen Thomas, with Myfanwy Thomas, *Under Storm's Wing* (Manchester: Carcanet, 1988).

R. George Thomas, ed.with a foreword by Myfanwy Thomas, *Letters to Helen Thomas: and an Appendix of Seven Letters to Harry and Jane Hooton* (Manchester: Carcanet, 2000).

R. George Thomas, *Edward Thomas: A Portrait* (Oxford: Clarendon Press, 1985).

ACKNOWLEDGEMENTS

Many thanks to Chloe Garner and the Ledbury Poetry Festival for commissioning 'And you, Helen'; other warm words of gratitude to Charlotte Hodes for the loveliest of collaborations; to Kristina Pulejkova for her expertise working on the accompanying animation; to Roger Walton for his vision and design; to Tony Rudolf, friend and first reader; to Emma Harding, for her generosity and companionship in research as we explored Helen's life together, and especially for taking me to Steep; to Hester Jones, Pam Windsor, John Lucas, Judith Palmer, Sarah Corbett, Ralph Pite, George Szirtes, Mick Felton, Nick Dear, Alison Brackenbury and David Morley, who at various points have all borne my current obsession with interest and forbearance.

Thanks to Alison Harvey at the Edward Thomas Archive, Cardiff University Library: Special Collections and Archives for help in my initial discovery of the holdings and ensuing assistance with permissions to repring photographs of Helen Thomas, and other objects from the archive; also to The Bodleian Libraries, The University of Oxford, and Mrs Rosemary Vellender for kind permission to reproduce the manuscript (MS. Don.d.28, fol.36r) 'And You, Helen'.

This book is for my mother, Angela and her twin James, and my cousins, and their families, all formerly – if some also presently – Thomases: Ruaraidh, Hamish and Pippa. It is also in memory of my children's grandmother, Brenda Breen. And it is for Eira and Felix, with all my love, and with thanks for allowing me sometimes to steal time, and to learn to look again.

Deryn Rees-Jones teaches literature at the University of Liverpool where she is Professor of Poetry. Her most recent collection of poems, *Burying the Wren* (Seren, 2012), was shortlisted for the Welsh Book of the Year and the T.S. Eliot Prize.

Charlotte Hodes is a painter and Professor in Fine Art at London College of Fashion, University of the Arts London. She won the Jerwood Drawing Prize in 2006 and has held solo exhibitions at the Wallace Collection London (2007), Marlborough Gallery (2009) and jaggedart (2014)